Oatmeal Cookbook

Delicious Oatmeal Recipes Made Easy

Table of Contents

Introduction

I want to thank you for purchasing this book, 'Oatmeal Cookbook: Delicious Oatmeal Recipes Made Easy.'

Despite their widespread praise by nutritionists and bodybuilders alike, oats have a humble origin. They were the last of the major cereal grains to be domesticated, around 3,000 years ago in Europe, and apparently originated as weeds that grew within cultivated fields of various other crops.

Part of the reason why people were slow to embrace oats is because they go rancid very quickly, due to the presence of natural fats and a fat dissolving enzyme present in the grain. As a result, they have to be processed immediately after harvesting. The fats in oats are relatively healthy, with a lipid breakdown of 21% saturated, 37% monounsaturated, and 43% polyunsaturated.

Greeks and Romans considered oats to be nothing more than a diseased version of wheat. Oats were a lowly horse food for the Romans, who scoffed at the "oat-eating barbarians", or those pesky Germanic tribes who eventually toppled the West Roman Empire.

Oats contain more soluble fiber than any other grain. Soluble fiber is the kind that dissolves in water, so the body turns it into a kind of thick, viscous gel, which moves very slowly through your body. One of the benefits is that your stomach stays fuller longer, providing satiety.

Soluble fiber also slows the absorption of glucose into the body, which means you're going to avoid those nasty sugar highs and lows. Last but not least, it inhibits the re-absorption of bile into the system, forcing your liver to get its cholesterol fix from your blood. This serves to lower your blood-serum cholesterol. See what the Romans were missing?

Oats also have anti-inflammatory properties, and have been clinically shown to help heal dry, itchy skin. Oats are also highly absorptive, hypoallergenic, and help to soften skin, if you're into that kind of thing. They have the best amino acid balance of all the cereal grains, and thus can be used as water-binding agents in skin care products.

Today, oats and oatmeal products are touted as a natural wonder food because of their high water-soluble fiber content, but oats have only become the darling of doctors and dieticians since the 1980s. Prior to the 1800's, oats were considered horse and cattle fodder while oatmeal was considered a food for the poor.

A

Apple Cinnamon Stovetop Oatmeal

Yield: 2

Ingredients:

- 3 tablespoons honey (or 2 tablespoons brown sugar), plus a little more to drizzle over the finished oatmeal
- 2 cups water
- 1 cup old fashioned oats (or gluten free oats)
- 1 medium crisp apple (about 1 ½ cups, diced)
- 1 teaspoon cinnamon
- ½ tablespoon unsalted butter
- ¼ teaspoon ground ginger
- ¼ teaspoon ground nutmeg
- pinch of salt
- ½ cup chopped walnuts (optional)
- ½ cup milk (optional)

Method:

1. First, melt the butter in a medium saucepan over medium high heat.
2. Add 1 cup of the apples, the honey or brown sugar, and sprinkle in the spices and salt. Cook for 2-3 minutes until the apples are softened.
3. Pour in the water, turn the heat up to high, and bring to a low boil. Add the oats and reduce the heat to medium/medium high. Cook, stirring occasionally for 3-5 more minutes.

4. Add the walnuts (if using), and continue cooking until most of the liquid is absorbed. Divide the oatmeal between two bowls, sprinkle each with the remaining apples, drizzle with a little more honey, and splash ¼ cup milk into each bowl.

Avocado and Poached Egg Oatmeal

Serves: 1

Ingredients:

- 2 tablespoons (15 g) shaved parmesan cheese
- 1 medium-large fresh egg
- 1 tablespoon (5 g) parsley, chopped
- 1 cup (236 ml) water
- ½ cup (60 g) rolled oats
- ½ avocado pitted, peeled, and sliced
- ground pepper to season
- pinch of salt

Method:

1. Start by combining oats, water, and salt in a medium pot and bring to a simmer over medium/low heat. Cook for about 10 minutes, until water is all absorbed.
2. Remove oatmeal from stove and stir in parmesan cheese. Cover to keep warm and set aside.
3. Bring another pot of water to a gentle simmer. Crack your egg in a small bowl, then gently lower into the hot water. Poach for about 3 minutes, then remove with a slotted spoon.
4. Spoon oatmeal into a serving bowl. Top with poached egg, sliced avocado, chopped parsley, and pepper. Serve warm.

Asparagus Oatmeal

Yield: 4 servings

Ingredients:

- 4 cups cold water
- 1 lb. asparagus spears (trimmed, cut into 5 pieces each on the diagonal, divided)
- 2 teaspoons fresh lemon juice
- ¾ teaspoon sea salt
- ½ teaspoon freshly ground black pepper
- 2 cups old-fashioned oats
- 2 scallions (green and white part, minced)
- 1 tablespoon fresh dill (finely chopped)
- 2 teaspoons extra-virgin olive oil

Method:

1. First, bring the water, all of the asparagus except the tips, lemon juice, salt, and pepper to a boil in a large saucepan.
2. Stir in the oats, asparagus tips, and scallions and reduce heat to medium. Cook, while stirring, until the oats and asparagus are fully cooked, about 6 minutes. Remove from heat and stir in the dill and olive oil.
3. Transfer the oatmeal to individual bowls and serve.

Note:

- This savory oatmeal recipe is a clever way to get vegetables at breakfast—and quite versatile. Mix and match different vegetables and fresh herbs in it, such as grape tomatoes and basil, diced bell peppers and oregano, or baby spinach and dill. And for a heartier meal, top each bowl with a poached egg.

Avena Caliente (Oatmeal and Milk Hot Drink)

Yield: 4 servings

Ingredients:

- 6 cloves
- 4 tablespoons of brown sugar (or more, to taste)
- 4 cups of water
- 4 cups of milk *(see notes)*
- 2 cinnamon sticks
- ½ cup (58 gr) oatmeal
- ¼ teaspoon of grated nutmeg
- ¼ teaspoon of salt (optional)

Method:

1. Start by mixing water, milk, salt and oatmeal and mix (in a blender) until the oatmeal is nearly dissolved.
2. In a 3 quart [3 lt] pot mix with cinnamon, cloves and nutmeg. Heat over medium heat, stir constantly.
3. Once it breaks the boil, lower heat and simmer until volume has reduced to ¾ of the original. Add sugar to taste
4. Serve warm.

Note:

- For a thicker, richer drink use evaporated milk. For a lighter drink, skim milk works very well. If you are lactose intolerant, or vegan, I have enjoyed it with almond milk.
- To sieve or not to sieve. You'll lose some fiber if you sieve this drink, but not as much as you'd think since

most will be blended in, it will only remove the large pieces left. Some like it like that. I'll leave it to you to decide.

Apple Pie Baked Oatmeal

Yield: 2-4

Ingredients:

- 2 tablespoons maple syrup
- 2 teaspoons cinnamon (ground)
- 2 apples (diced)
- 1 cup (120 g) rolled oats
- 1 cup (250 ml) boiling water
- 1 banana (sliced)
- ½ cup (80 g) raisins
- ¼ cup (65 ml) oat milk
- ¼ teaspoon nutmeg (ground)

Method:

1. First, preheat the oven to 180°C or 355°F.
2. Place the oats in a bowl and add boiling water (you have to cover the oats). Let stand for about 10 minutes. Then add the rest of the ingredients.
3. Mix well and place the oatmeal in a baking dish.
4. Bake for 30 minutes or until golden brown.

Notes:

- This recipe with 2 tablespoons ground cinnamon, but if it was too much, you can use only 2 teaspoons. If you love cinnamon, feel free to add more.

Almond Milk Oatmeal

Yield: 4 servings

Ingredients:

- 2 cups unsweetened almond milk
- 1 cup old-fashioned rolled oats
- ¼ teaspoon sea salt (or Himalayan salt)

Method:

1. First, bring almond milk and salt to a boil in medium saucepan over medium heat, stirring frequently.
2. Add oats; cook over medium-low heat, stirring frequently, for 3 to 5 minutes.
3. Let oatmeal stand for 1 minute before serving.

Notes:

- You can substitute 1 cup water and 1 cup unsweetened almond milk for 2 cups almond milk if you want a lighter version of this oatmeal.
- This recipe can also be microwaved easily. Place almond milk and oats in a large microwaveable bowl. (Make sure your bowl is big enough that the oatmeal doesn't boil over.) Cook for 2 minutes on high. Stir oatmeal. Cook an additional 2 minutes. Stir oatmeal. Cook an additional 2 to 3 minutes if needed.

Atole do Avena (Mexican Sweet Oatmeal)

Servings: 1

Ingredients:

- 3 cup milk (we use raw milk but you can use any full fat)
- 2 cup water
- 1 ½ cup old fashioned oats
- 1 bar of piloncillo
- 1 Mexican cinnamon stick

Method:

1. Start by cutting the piloncillo into small pieces.
2. Add the piloncillo to the water in a stockpot and allow it to dissolve on low heat.
3. Add the cinnamon and oats to the mixture, and stir in well. Use 1 C. of oats for a thinner drink, and 1 ½ for a thicker drink.
4. Bring to a boil over medium, reduce the heat, and then cover and allow the mixture to thicken (10 minutes).
5. Once oats have absorbed much of the water, then add in the milk and stir to combine well.
6. Simmer until the atole reaches the consistency you are looking for.

B

Blueberry Cheesecake Baked Oatmeal

Servings: 8

Ingredients:

- 4 cups old-fashioned oats
- 4 cups milk
- 3 medium-large eggs
- 3 tablespoons butter (melted)
- 2 teaspoons vanilla
- 1 ½ teaspoons baking powder
- 1 cup frozen organic blueberries
- 1 package (8 oz) cream cheese (softened)
- 1 cup packed brown sugar
- ¾ teaspoon salt
- ½ cup blueberry preserves
- 1/3 cup granulated sugar

Method:

1. First, heat oven to 350°F.
2. Spray 13x9-inch (3-quart) baking dish with cooking spray.
3. Stir together oats, brown sugar, baking powder and salt in large bowl.
4. Beat milk, 2 of the eggs, melted butter and vanilla in large bowl with whisk. Add milk mixture and frozen blueberries to oat mixture; gently stir to combine.
5. Pour into baking dish; let stand 15 minutes.

6. In medium bowl, beat cream cheese, granulated sugar and remaining egg with whisk until smooth. Spoon cream cheese mixture by tablespoonfuls evenly onto oat mixture. Next to each spoonful of cream cheese mixture, place a spoonful of blueberry preserves. Cut through mixture several times with knife for marbled design.
7. Bake 40 to 50 minutes or until center is set. Let stand 15 minutes before serving.

Notes:

- Fresh blueberries can be substituted for the frozen blueberries in this recipe.
- Letting the oat mixture stand before topping it with the cream cheese allows it to thicken enough so the cream cheese doesn't sink to the bottom of the baking dish.

Banana Oatmeal Cookies

Servings: 18

Ingredients:

- 3 ripe bananas (mashed well)
- 2 cups oatmeal (either quick or old-fashioned work in this recipe)
- 1 cup dates
- 1 teaspoon cinnamon
- 1/3 cup unsweetened applesauce

Method:

1. Start by soaking the dates in 1 cup hot water for 10 minutes to soften. Drain dates from soaking liquid.
2. Preheat oven to 350 degrees.
3. In a food processor, mix together bananas, apple sauce, dates, and cinnamon until well combined. Add in oats and process until just combined.
4. Drop by rounded tablespoons unto a cookie sheet and bake at 350 for 15 minutes.

Notes:

- If you do not have a food processor, chop up the soaked dates, and then mash together with bananas, applesauce, cinnamon and oats. You will have a chunkier, but still delicious Banana Breakfast Cookie. Add mini dark chocolate chips to make these extra special.
- If you can't find whole dates, raisins will work as well (and the raisins do not need soaked.

- You can use quick cook oats or old-fashioned oatmeal for this recipe.
- If you are using dates, be sure they have not been coated with sugar. Dates are plenty sweet on their own.
- Reserve the date soaking liquid to add to oatmeal recipes or smoothies for naturals sweetness.

Butterscotch Oatmeal

Servings: 1

Ingredients:

- 2 cups milk
- 1 cup quick oats
- 1 medium-large egg
- 1/3 cup packed brown sugar
- ¼ teaspoon salt
- 2 teaspoons butter (optional)

Method:

1. First, whisk together the milk, egg, brown sugar, and salt in a small saucepan.
2. Turn the heat on to medium, and don't go higher than that the whole time you are cooking otherwise it will turn out grainy.
3. Mix in the oats. Stir occasionally. When the oatmeal begins to bubble, cook and stir until thick.
4. When it has reached the consistency you like, remove from heat, and stir in butter until melted.
5. I usually let it sit off the heat with a lid on for a couple minutes so that it gets nice and thick.
6. Serve with milk and fruit!

Basic Oatmeal

Servings: 2

Ingredients:

- 1 cup old-fashioned rolled oats
- 1 cup milk
- 1 cup water
- 1 teaspoon honey
- ½ teaspoon ground cinnamon
- 1/8 teaspoon kosher salt
- desired toppings (such as sliced almonds, peanut butter, or fresh fruit)

Method:

1. Start by combining oats, milk, water, salt, and cinnamon in a medium saucepan. Bring to a boil, then reduce heat to low.
2. Simmer uncovered for 3 to 5 minutes until thickened, stirring occasionally. Remove from heat and let cool slightly.
3. Divide equally between two bowls. Drizzle each serving with ½ teaspoon honey.
4. Add additional desired toppings and serve.

Beets and Carrots Oatmeal

Servings: 1-2

Ingredients:

- 2 cups water or milk
- 1 cup organic old-fashioned oats
- 1 organic carrot (peeled and shredded)
- 1 teaspoon cinnamon
- ½ organic red beet (peeled and shredded)
- ¼ teaspoon cloves
- 1/8 teaspoon nutmeg
- 2 tablespoons raisins (optional)

Method:

1. First, bring water to a boil in a medium saucepan over medium heat.
2. Add the oats, beets, carrots, cinnamon, cloves, nutmeg and raisins, stir and bring back to boil then turn heat to low.
3. Let cook for 10 minutes or until all the water is evaporated, stirring occasionally. Let cool slightly.
4. *For baby,* add oatmeal to blender or food processor and puree until smooth.
5. *For toddler,* add any other toppings and serve.

C

Classic Oatmeal

Servings: 1

Ingredients:

- 1 cup milk
- 1 tablespoon unsalted butter
- ½ cup old fashioned oats
- ¼ teaspoon salt
- mix-ins, as desired

Method:

1. First, mix together the oats, milk, salt, and butter into a small saucepan and cook on medium heat.
2. Stir the mixture until it begins to bubble and the oats soften. This should take about 5 minutes and the mixture should look thick and creamy. Add more milk or water if you prefer a thinner oatmeal.
3. Add in any mix-ins that you desire. Sugar, cocoa powder, peanut butter, and mashed peanut butter make great sweet mix-ins to add now. Alternatively, you can consider, cheese and herbs for savory oatmeal.
4. Pour the cooked oats into a bowl. Add in any other mix-ins as desired such as nuts, dried berries, or bacon.

Chocolate-Raspberry Oatmeal

Servings: 10 crepes

Ingredients:

- 3 cups unsweetened almond milk
- 2 tablespoons unsweetened cocoa powder
- 1 ½ cups regular rolled oats
- 1 cup fresh red raspberries
- ¼ teaspoon salt
- 4 teaspoons sugar-free chocolate-flavor syrup (optional)

Method:

5. First, stir together oats, cocoa powder and salt in a medium saucepan. Stir in almond milk. Bring to boiling over medium heat, stirring occasionally; reduce heat.
6. Simmer, uncovered, 5 to 7 minutes or until thickened, stirring occasionally. Cover. Remove from heat; let stand 2 minutes.
7. Divide oatmeal mixture among four serving bowls. Top each serving with ¼ cup of the raspberries. If desired, drizzle each serving with 1 teaspoon of the chocolate syrup.
8. Serve and enjoy!

Coffee Oatmeal

Yield: 1

Ingredients:

- 1 pinch salt
- 1 tablespoon honey or maple syrup
- 1 teaspoon vanilla extract
- ¾ cup milk of your choice (almond milk lends a nice nutty flavor; half and half or cream makes it rich)
- ½ cup rolled oats (not quick oats)
- ¼ cup brewed coffee

Method:

Stovetop Oats:

1. First, add the oats, milk, coffee, and salt to a small (1-quart) saucepan and cover.
2. Bring to a simmer over medium heat, stirring occasionally until the oatmeal thickens, about 5 minutes.
3. Add more milk or water as needed until the oats are tender and at your desired consistency.
4. Stir in the honey or maple syrup and vanilla during the last minute of cooking.
5. Remove from the heat and enjoy immediately or add more mix-ins.

Overnight Oats:

1. If you don't plan to heat up your oatmeal in the morning (which cooks off some of the liquid),

decrease your milk to ½ cup and your coffee by a tablespoon or so.

2. Combine all ingredients and place in refrigerator overnight. You can use a small Pyrex dish with a lid because you can eat right out of it in the morning.
3. This method also works with steel-cut oats even better, because you don't have to spend 30 minutes waiting for them to simmer and soften on the stove. You wake up and they're already ready for you!
4. And if you're going to do overnight oats, why not keep a jar of iced coffee in your refrigerator at all times.
5. Those few sips of coffee left over at the bottom of the pot that you don't have time to drink before running out the door might seem like nothing at the time, but....
6. Pour them into a jar every day for two weeks and you will be thankful when you wake up hung over on Saturday morning and realize with despair that you are out of coffee and the world is ending, because, oh wait! It isn't, because you have two full cups of coffee in your refrigerator.

Notes:

Our favorite coffee oatmeal variations! Just add these to the basic recipe above, or mix and match:

- *Mocha oatmeal:* add 1 tablespoon cocoa powder.
- *Peanut butter pie oatmeal:* add 1 tablespoon cocoa powder and 1 tablespoon peanut butter.
- *Oatmeal cookie oatmeal:* add 1 tablespoon cinnamon, 1 tablespoon maple syrup, and a handful of raisins.

- *Pecan pie oatmeal:* add 2 tablespoons maple syrup, 1 tablespoon cinnamon, and a handful of chopped pecans.
- *Nut butter and jelly oatmeal:* Add 2 tablespoons almond butter and a handful of fresh blueberries or 1 tablespoon blueberry jam.
- *Peanut butter and banana oatmeal:* Add 1 tablespoon peanut butter, 1 tablespoon cinnamon, and a sliced banana.
- *Tropical oatmeal:* Add a splash of coconut milk (or cook your oatmeal in coconut milk), a handful of coconut flakes, and your favorite fresh fruit like raspberries, mango, or kiwi

Carrot Cake Oatmeal

Serves: 1

Ingredients:

- 2 tablespoons walnuts (toasted, chopped)
- 1 tablespoon brown sugar (plus more to taste)
- 1 tablespoon butter (plus more to taste)
- 1 carrot
- 1 pinch salt
- ½ cup rolled oats
- ¼ teaspoon vanilla extract
- 1/8 teaspoon cinnamon
- 1 tablespoon raisins (optional)

Method:

1. First, peel the carrot and grate it into a small saucepan.
2. Add 1 cup of water and the pinch of salt. Bring to a boil over high heat. Stir in the oats, vanilla, cinnamon, and raisins (if using). Adjust the heat to maintain a steady simmer and cook, stirring frequently, until the oats and carrot are tender, about 5 minutes.
3. Take the pan off the heat. Stir in the brown sugar. Transfer to a bowl. Dot the top with bits of the butter.
4. Sprinkle with more brown sugar, if you like, and top with the walnuts. Serve hot.

Variations:

- *Make it creamy:* Stir in a tablespoon or two of cream, half-and-half, or whole milk along with the sugar.

- *Make it creamier:* Use whole milk instead of water to cook the oatmeal. Be careful and don't let it quite come to a boil if you choose this option.
- *Bring on the coconut:* Stir in a tablespoon or two of coconut milk along with the sugar for lots of creaminess and a lovely note of coconut flavor.
- *Bring on more coconut:* Stir in or top with grated or shredded coconut.
- *Make it nuttier:* Stir in a tablespoon of almond butter along with the sugar.
- *Swap the nuts:* Try roasted chopped almonds, cashews, or pecans instead of walnuts.
- *Swap the fruit:* Use dried cranberries, dried blueberries, currants, chopped dates or dried figs instead of raisins or currants.
- *Frost it:* Sweeten a tablespoon or two of whipped cream cheese with brown sugar and dollop it on top of the finished carrot cake oatmeal as a sort of "frosting."

Crunchy Quinoa Baked Oatmeal with Caramelized Strawberries and Coconut

Servings: 4

Ingredients:

- 3 tablespoons unsalted butter (melted and cooled)
- 2 tablespoons brown sugar
- 2 tablespoons unsweetened flaked coconut
- 2 teaspoons vanilla extract
- 2 tablespoons butter
- 1 ½ cups old-fashioned rolled oats
- 1 1/3 cups canned lite coconut milk
- 1 medium-large egg
- 1-pint strawberries (stems removed)
- 1 teaspoon baking powder
- ¾ cups uncooked quinoa (rinsed)
- ½ teaspoon cinnamon
- 1/3 cup loosely packed brown sugar
- ¼ teaspoon salt
- ¼ teaspoon salt

Method:

1. First, preheat oven to 375 degrees F.
2. Combine oats, rinsed quinoa, sugar, baking powder, cinnamon and salt in a large bowl. Mix well to combine.
3. In a smaller bowl, whisk together coconut milk, egg, vanilla extract and melted butter. Add the wet

ingredients to the dry, then spread in a small baking dish or pie plate. (We used 9-inch in diameter.) Bake for 30-35 minutes, or until golden on top and set.

4. While baking, heat a skillet over medium-low heat and add butter.
5. Add strawberries with a pinch of salt, tossing to coat. Cook until slightly golden then sprinkle with brown sugar and stir. Cook a few minutes more until soft and caramelly.
6. To toast coconut, add to a small saucepan over medium heat and stir for 5-6 minutes until golden. Remove immediately.
7. Top oatmeal with strawberries and coconut and whipped cream if desired. You can add a little extra splash of milk too!

Creme Brulee Oatmeal

Servings: 4

Ingredients:

- 3 cups water
- 2 cups quick-cooking oats
- 2 bananas (sliced)
- 1 cup instant vanilla pudding or ready-made vanilla pudding
- ½ teaspoon ground cinnamon
- ½ teaspoon kosher salt (¼ teaspoon table salt)
- ¼ cup brown sugar

Method:

1. If using instant pudding, cook according to package instructions.
2. Bring water to boil, stir in quick-cooking oats and cook until thickened, about 1-2 minutes.
3. For thinner oatmeal, add just a bit more water. Divide oatmeal amongst 4 oven-proof bowls.
4. Place oven rack near top and turn on broiler. Top each bowl with vanilla pudding and banana slices.
5. Sprinkle brown sugar and cinnamon on top. Place in broiler until sugar melts and begins to bubble.

Chia Seed Oatmeal

Servings: 1

Ingredients:

- 1 tablespoon chia seeds
- 1 tablespoon flaxseeds (finely ground)
- 1 tablespoon agave nectar
- ½ cup instant oatmeal
- ¼ cup raisins
- ¼ cup walnut pieces
- ¼ cup milk

Method:

1. First, combine the oatmeal and 1 cup water.
2. Microwave on full power for 2 minutes or until the oats are cooked. Add the chia seeds, ground flaxseeds, raisins, walnuts and agave nectar.
3. Let sit 3 to 4 minutes. Stir in the milk.
4. Serve and enjoy!

Note:

- Most people like their oatmeal with a pinch of salt. If you do, add it before microwaving.

Chilled Swiss Oatmeal

Servings: 1-2

Ingredients:

- 2 tablespoons dried cranberries (fruit juice sweetened)
- 1 tablespoon roasted almonds (chopped)
- 1 cup uncooked old-fashioned rolled oats
- ½ cup unsweetened vanilla almond milk + 2 splashes
- ½ cup plain 2% Greek yogurt (substitute soy, almond or coconut milk yogurt if needed)
- ½ cored pink lady apple (chopped into small pieces)
- ½ of a ripe banana (chopped into small pieces)
- ½ teaspoon vanilla
- sprinkle of cinnamon
- chia seeds (for sprinkling on top)
- maple syrup (for drizzling)

Method:

1. Start by placing oats, milk, yogurt, cranberries, apple, banana, vanilla and cinnamon in a medium-sized bowl, soak (covered) in the refrigerator overnight.
2. In the morning, add a splash or two of almond milk and stir the mixture. Portion out a serving and sprinkle almonds, chia seeds and a drizzle of maple syrup over the top. Enjoy!

Caramel Oatmeal Chewies

Servings: 2 ½ dozen

Ingredients:

- 12 tablespoons (1 ½ sticks) butter or margarine, melted
- 2 cup (12-oz. pkg.) semi-sweet chocolate chips
- 1 ¾ cup quick or old-fashioned oats (uncooked)
- 1 ¾ cup all-purpose flour (divided)
- 1 cup nuts (chopped)
- 1 cup caramel ice cream topping
- ¾ cup firmly packed brown sugar
- ½ teaspoon baking soda
- ¼ teaspoon salt (optional)

Method:

1. First, heat oven to 350° F.
2. Grease bottom of 13x9-inch metal baking pan.
3. In large bowl, combine oats, 1 ½ cups flour, sugar, baking soda and salt. Stir in butter; mix well. Reserve 1 cup oat mixture; press remaining oat mixture onto bottom of baking pan.
4. Bake 12 to 15 minutes or until golden brown. Sprinkle with chips and nuts. Mix caramel topping with remaining flour in small bowl; drizzle over nuts to within ¼ inch of pan edges. Sprinkle with reserved oat mixture.
5. Continue baking 18 to 22 minutes or until golden brown. Cool in pan on wire rack; refrigerate until firm. Cut into bars.

Cranberry Almond Oatmeal

Servings: 1

Ingredients:

- 1 cup milk of choice, or water
- ½ cup rolled oats
- ½ ripe banana
- ½ teaspoon almond extract
- ¼ cup dried cranberries
- ¼ teaspoon vanilla extract
- pinch of salt
- almonds

Method:

1. First, bring milk (I ½ c original almond milk and ½ c water) to a boil, add oats, and reduce heat to medium. (If you'd like to add flax or chia seeds, do so now.)
2. Mash banana thoroughly and add to the oatmeal. Also add cranberries at this time.
3. Once more of the liquid has absorbed, add vanilla extract, almond extract, and salt. Stir.
4. When you're pleased with the consistency of the oatmeal, transfer to a bowl.
5. Serve with another splash of your milk of choice, almonds, and any other additional toppings. (shredded coconut, nuts, etc.)

Caribbean Oats Porridge

Servings: 8-10

Ingredients:

- 3 cups water (separated)
- 1 cup rolled oats
- 1 (3-inch) cinnamon stick
- ½ teaspoon nutmeg (freshly grated)
- ¼ cup raisins (rinsed)
- sugar and milk to taste

Method:

1. First, soak the oats in 1 cup of water for 4 minutes.
2. Bring 2 cups of water and the cinnamon stick to a boil while the oats are soaking.
3. Add the soaked oats along with any residual soaking liquid to the water when it begins to boil.
4. Stir in the rinsed raisins and reduce the heat to low. Cook covered for 5 to 6 minutes or until the mixture becomes very thick.
5. Remove from the heat and remove the cinnamon stick. Stir in the nutmeg, along with sugar and milk to taste.

Tips:

- Oats porridge isn't just for breakfast or a snack. Add your choice of vegetables to serve it as a side dish. Small chunks of carrots work well alone or combined with peas or potatoes.

- Serve cooked porridge with a dollop of yogurt on top and drizzled with honey and optional chopped nuts, such as walnuts or almonds.

Recipe variations:

- Add pieces of fruit like green bananas, plantains, oranges, or breadfruit to the cooked porridge.
- Use coconut milk or sweetened condensed milk in place of cow's milk for a sweeter flavor. If you're worried about fat content, use non-dairy milk but the porridge will be thinner.
- Use quick-cooking oats in place of rolled oats but adjust the cooking time based on the package instructions.

Creamy Cardamom Oatmeal

Servings: 1

Ingredients:

- 2 cups whole oats
- 2 cups coconut milk
- 2 cups water
- 1 teaspoon cardamom
- ¼ cup coconut sugar

Method:

1. First, in a covered saucepan, bring the water and coconut milk to a boil.
2. Add coconut sugar, vanilla, cardamom, salt, and oatmeal.
3. Reduce heat and simmer until the extra liquid is absorbed, about 15 minutes.
4. Serve warm and enjoy!

D

Date Sweetened Oatmeal

Servings: 1

Ingredients:

Oatmeal:

- 2 pitted dates (chopped)
- 1 ½ cups of unsweetened almond milk
- ½ cup of steel cut oats
- splash of vanilla extract
- sprinkle of cinnamon

Toppings:

- raw walnuts
- pepitas
- brazil nuts
- golden berries

Method:

1. First, boil milk in a medium sauce pan.
2. Once milk is boiling, add oats and chopped dates to pan, stir & cover.
3. Let the oats simmer for 15-20 minutes (or until all liquid is absorbed).
4. Pour in bowl of your choice, top with vanilla extract, cinnamon and any of the other toppings.

E

Eggnog Overnight Oats - Vegan

Yield: 1

Ingredients:

- 1-2 tablespoons pomegranate arils
- 1 teaspoon chia seeds
- ¾ cup eggnog (or ½ cup eggnog + ¼ cup unsweetened almond milk)
- ½ cup rolled oats
- sprinkle of cinnamon
- freshly grated nutmeg (for topping)
- ½ scoop vanilla protein powder (optional)

Method:

1. First, combine oats, eggnog, protein powder (if using), chia seeds and cinnamon in small container, seal with a lid and place in the fridge overnight.
2. You'll notice that the protein powder, oats and chia seeds soak up a lot of the liquid so you may want to add a little more eggnog or milk to thin it out a bit before serving.
3. Top oats with pomegranate arils and a sprinkle of freshly grated nutmeg and enjoy.
4. Traditionally overnight oats are served cold, but you can certainly heat them up if you'd like.

Note:

- For the eggnog, you can use whatever type of eggnog you have on hand.
- You can add vanilla protein powder for a little extra protein. If you don't do protein powder, you can leave this out or add in ¼ cup yogurt for extra protein.
- No eggnog? No problem. Just use ¾ cup of almond milk and add in ½ teaspoon of cinnamon, ¼ teaspoon of freshly ground nutmeg and ¼ teaspoon rum extract (optional).

Egg White Oatmeal

Servings: 1

Ingredients:

- 2 teaspoons honey
- 1 cup almond milk
- ½ teaspoon cinnamon
- ½ cup old fashioned oats
- ¼ liquid egg whites
- ¼ teaspoon ginger

Method:

1. Start by heating ¾ cup almond milk in pan.
2. Once almond milk is boiling, add in oats and cook on medium heat for 8-10 minutes until almost all of the milk is absorbed.
3. Once all of the almond milk is just about absorbed in oatmeal, stir in egg whites, cinnamon, ginger + honey and remaining ¼ cup almond milk.
4. Stir constantly for 2 minutes over medium heat until everything is combined and egg whites have cooked. The oatmeal should be smooth and pull away from the pan when stirring.
5. Serve with nut butter or fresh berries of your choice!

Tips for making Egg White Oatmeal:

- Make sure you stir the oatmeal consistently when you pour in the egg whites. If you don't stir the egg whites, they will cook up unevenly and you'll wind up with oats and scrambled egg whites. I promise you don't want this!

- Load up on the toppings! The honey, cinnamon and ginger definitely add flavor - but fresh fruit and nut butters make this egg white oatmeal so much better!

F

Flaxseed Oatmeal with Blueberries

Servings: 4

Ingredients:

- 3 cups water
- 3 tablespoons ground flaxseed
- 2 cups old-fashioned rolled oats
- 1 ½ tablespoons butter
- 1 tablespoon fresh lemon juice
- 1 teaspoon raw sugar
- 1 cup frozen blueberries
- 1 tablespoon blueberry preserves
- ½ teaspoon grated lemon rind
- ¼ cup whole milk
- ¼ cup coarsely chopped pecans (toasted)
- 1/8 teaspoon kosher salt

Method:

1. Start by boiling 3 cups water.
2. Stir in oats, flaxseed, and salt. Reduce heat to medium-low; cook for 6 minutes or until tender, stirring frequently. Stir in milk and butter.
3. Meanwhile, combine blueberries and next 4 ingredients (through sugar) in a microwave-safe bowl; microwave at high for 1 ½ minutes, stirring every 30 seconds.

4. Divide oatmeal among 4 bowls. Top with blueberries and pecans.

Fried Oatmeal

Servings: 4

Ingredients:

- 1 cup water
- ½ cup old-fashioned oats
- 1/8 teaspoon salt
- nonstick spray
- butter (optional)
- syrup butter, fruit, peanut butter (optional toppings)

Method:

1. First, bring oats, water, and salt to boil in a small pot.
2. Lower Heat. Cook five minutes, stirring constantly until a thick consistency is reached.
3. Place oatmeal in square baking pan and spread evenly.
4. Cover and refrigerate at least 2-3 hours.
5. When cool, cut oatmeal into eight equal pieces.
6. Heat a skillet over medium-high heat, spray with nonstick spray.
7. Carefully lift oatmeal pieces out of the dish and onto the pan. Sear both sides of the oatmeal square - it takes a while because of all the moisture in the oatmeal. Add more nonstick spray as needed.
8. When oatmeal pieces are fairly seared, feel free to add a little butter (along with some more nonstick spray). Butter burns at a much lower temperature, so don't do this until the end.

G

Ginger Mushroom Oatmeal

Servings: 3-4

Ingredients:

- 8 oz. cremini mushrooms
- 3 cups water
- 1 cup steel cut oats
- 1 cup vegetable stock
- 1 tablespoon butter
- 1-inch fresh ginger (peeled and minced)
- dash of soy sauce
- pinch of red pepper flakes
- scallions, garnish
- soft-boiled eggs

Method:

1. First, add water and stock in a medium pot and bring to a simmer.
2. Add steel cut oats and turn heat down to low. Let oats simmer until they are tender, about 30 minutes. Stir regularly and add more water if the pot looks dry at any point.
3. *For mushrooms,* add butter to a large skillet. Slice mushrooms and add to the skillet. Cook over medium heat until the mushrooms lose their liquid and cook down, about 5 minutes. Then add ginger and a dash of soy sauce. Remove from heat.

4. *For soft-boiled eggs,* bring an inch of water to a rapid boil in a pot with a lid. Gently add eggs to the water (they won't be covered, it's fine). Return cover and let the eggs cook rapidly for 6.5 minutes. Then drain eggs and rinse with cold water for 30 seconds. Then carefully peel eggs starting with the fatter end of the egg.
5. Once oats are done, stir in half of the diced mushrooms. Divide oatmeal between bowls and top with extra mushrooms, scallions, and egg. Enjoy!

Gingerbread Oatmeal

Servings: 8

Ingredients:

Custard sauce:

- 8 egg yolks
- 2 cups whole milk
- 2 cups half & half
- ½ teaspoon corn starch
- ¼ cup sugar

Matcha ricotta filling:

- 4 ½ cups water (divided)
- 2 teaspoons molasses
- 1 teaspoon ground ginger
- 1 cup steel cut oats or organic steel cut oats
- ½ teaspoon sea salt
- ½ teaspoon ground allspice
- ½ teaspoon ground cinnamon
- ½ teaspoon nutmeg
- ½ teaspoon ground cloves
- ¼ cup brown sugar

Method:

Oatmeal:

1. First, soak oats in 2 cups water overnight. Drain before using.

2. Bring 2 ½ cups water and salt to a boil. Add soaked oats, stir till boiling.
3. Cover and simmer for 20 minutes, stirring occasionally with your spurtle.
4. In last 5 minutes of cooking time, add molasses, spices and brown sugar.

Custard sauce:

1. Bring milk, half and half and sugar to scalding (not boiling). Whisk in corn starch.
2. Meanwhile, whisk the egg yolks. Add ½ cup of the hot milk to the eggs, whisking rapidly. Slowly pour eggs into pan, whisking continuously.
3. Switch to a wooden spoon, stir gently and continuously until custard sauce has thickened slightly. Do not let it boil or eggs will curdle and separate.
4. Spoon over cooked oatmeal.

Greek Oatmeal

Servings: 1

Ingredients:

- 2 tablespoons hummus *(see note)*
- ½ cup unsweetened milk (preferably soy)
- ¼ cup water
- ¼ cup quick-cooking steel cut oats
- 1/8 cup of diced red onion or ¼ teaspoon onion powder
- 1/8 teaspoon salt
- handful of spinach (cut/ripped in strips)
- ½ cup grated zucchini or yellow squash (optional)

Optional toppings:

- handful sliced kalamati olives
- handful tomatoes (cherry or sun-dried)
- diced cucumber
- crumbled feta (vegans, try this)
- toasted pine nuts
- tahini
- olive oil
- parsley or basil

Method:

1. Start by sautéing onion in a bit of oil until translucent.
2. Add water and milk and bring to a boil. Add oats and zucchini, and reduce heat to medium.

3. Once more of the liquid has absorbed, add hummus, some freshly ground black pepper, and salt. Stir.
4. Once your oatmeal has reached the desired consistency, turn off the heat and add spinach, stirring it in. The heat from the oatmeal will wilt it.
5. Transfer to a bowl. Top with any or all of the optional toppings you'd prefer.

Golden Milk Oatmeal

Servings: 4

Ingredients:

- 2 cups old-fashioned oats
- 2 teaspoons ground turmeric
- 1 ½ teaspoons ground ginger
- 1 15-oz. can full-fat coconut milk
- ½ teaspoon cinnamon
- 3/8 teaspoon salt
- 2 tablespoons raw honey, plus more for drizzling (optional)

Method:

1. First, stir together 1 ¼ cups water and all ingredients in a medium pan. Bring to a boil.
2. Reduce heat to medium-low and simmer, stirring once or twice, until liquid has absorbed and oats are creamy, about 5 minutes.
3. Divide among 4 bowls; drizzle with additional honey, if desired.

Garlic Oats with Fried Egg

Servings: 1

Ingredients:

For the Oats:

- 2 – 3 cloves garlic (minced)
- 2 teaspoons basil (chopped)
- 2 cups water
- 1 teaspoon oil
- 1 cup quick cooking oats
- ¼ cup mild cheddar (grated)

For the eggs:

- 2 medium-large eggs
- 1 teaspoon olive oil
- ½ teaspoon paprika or chili powder
- salt and pepper to taste

Method:

Cook the Oats:

1. First, heat a teaspoon of oil in a pan and add minced garlic.
2. Sauté the garlic for 15 seconds and add oats. Stir the oats for a few seconds and add all the water, salt and pepper.
3. Bring this to a quick boil, and simmer for 3-4 minutes, by which time, the mixture would have thickened up into a porridge like consistency and the oats will be cooked.

4. Adjust the consistency by adding more water if required. Just before taking oats off the stove, add cheese and basil and mix.

Fry the eggs:

1. In a non-stick pan, add the olive oil and fry the eggs one by one. Top each egg with salt and paprika or chili powder.

Assemble and Serve:

1. To serve, divide the oats equally into two bowls. Top each bowl with a fried egg, sprinkle with more paprika and chopped coriander.

H

Healthy Snickerdoodle Baked Oatmeal with Cinnamon Chips

Serves: 2

Ingredients:

- 4 packets stevia or 8 teaspoons sugar
- 2 eggs or 6 tablespoons liquid egg whites
- 2 tablespoon cinnamon chips plus a few extras for topping *(see note)*
- 2 teaspoons cinnamon
- 1 cup rolled oats
- ½ teaspoon nutmeg
- ½ teaspoon baking powder
- ¼ teaspoon salt
- 2/3 cup plain greek-style yogurt
- 2/3 cup milk (you can use 1% milk, soy or almond milk)

Method:

1. First, preheat oven to 375°F / 190°C.
2. Combine oats, cinnamon, nutmeg, baking powder, salt, and stevia in a small bowl.
3. In a medium bowl, whisk together yogurt, milk, and eggs.
4. Add dry ingredients to wet ingredients and stir until well combined. Fold in cinnamon chips.

5. Spray a medium baking dish with cooking spray (I used a 6 x 9-inch dish, but anything similar will work).
6. Transfer oatmeal mixture to prepared dish and bake for approximately 20-25 minutes, or until top is golden brown and center is just about set. If you don't like the baked oatmeal to get too dried out, pull it out of the oven when it might still be a little soft in the center. That way, as it cools, it firms slightly but still retains lots of gooey moisture.
7. Remove from oven, allow to cool for at least 5 minutes, drizzle with maple syrup and additional cinnamon chips, and dig in!

Recipe tips:

- Cinnamon chips are often found in the baking aisle around the holidays, or you can order them online! If you have trouble finding them, you can substitute with white chocolate chips, regular chocolate chips, berries, raisins, or just leave them out entirely.

High Protein Oatmeal

Serving: 1

Ingredients:

- 1 tablespoon flax meal
- 1 scoop collagen omit for vegan
- ¾ cup unsweetened almond milk or as much milk as you need to thicken
- ½ cup gluten free rolled oats
- ½ tablespoon chia seeds
- ½ tablespoon cinnamon
- ¼ cup vanilla protein powder
- 1/8 cup powdered peanut butter

Method:

For instant oats:

1. Place all ingredients except milk in a mason jar or plastic bag.
2. When ready to eat, add milk, stir, and heat for 1:30 to 2:00 minutes in the microwave. Top with fruit.

For overnight oats:

1. Place all ingredients in a mason jar.
2. Stir the ingredients together, cover and place in the refrigerator overnight. Eat the next day. Fruit can be added the night before or day of.

I

Instant Pot Oatmeal

Serves: 2-3

Ingredients:

- 1 cup steel cut oats (or regular oats)
- 2 ½ to 3 cups water, depending how thick you like your oatmeal

Topping choices:

- strawberries
- bananas
- blueberries
- apples
- pears
- chopped dates
- cinnamon
- flax seed, coconut flakes
- peanut butter
- etc.

Method:

1. First, add steel cut oats and water to the Instant Pot. Place the lid on the Instant Pot and press the "Porridge" button (or Manual/Pressure Cook). Make sure it's set to 6 minutes, and turn knob on the top of the lid to Sealing (not venting).

2. The Instant Pot will turn on and start to build pressure. After about 10 minutes, the timer will automatically set to 6 minutes.
3. After the 6 minutes are done, it will need to sit for an additional 6-8 minutes to release the pressure (you will see the L0:02, etc. on the screen which means it is releasing pressure on low heat). When the pressure is released, remove the lid. (Note: If the pressure is not released, you won't be able to open it).
4. Add the oatmeal to a bowl, and add toppings of choice. It will store in an airtight container in the fridge for 5-6 days.

Notes:

- You may need to experiment to see how you prefer your oatmeal consistency. 3 cups of water will lend to a more watery oatmeal, but 2 ½ cups water (or even a little less) will result in a firmer oatmeal.
- This recipe makes 2-3 servings, depending on the amount of toppings you add. You can easily double the recipe and use the same cooking time.

J

Japanese Savory Oatmeal

Serves: 2

Ingredients:

- 3-4 sprigs of parsley (stripped and chopped)
- 4 squares of wasabi seaweed snacks (could also use 1 toasted nori sheet), crushed
- 1 cup rolled oats
- 1 small sweet potato (baked and diced)
- 1 lg. spring onion (diced)
- 1 teaspoon sesame seeds
- pat of butter or oil
- soy sauce (to drizzle)
- sesame oil (to drizzle)
- sriracha (to drizzle)

Method:

1. First, butter in a medium saucepan over medium heat until butter begins to brown.
2. Add oats, and cook until edges begin to brown and a toasty aroma is exuded, stirring regularly. Then add 2 cups of water. Cover and bring heat to a boil, then reduce heat to a low simmer. Cook 10-15 minutes, or until water is absorbed and oats are tender.
3. When oats are finished cooking, divide among two bowls. Drizzle each with soy sauce.
4. Add ½ sweet potato to each bowl, and drizzle the sweet potato with toasted sesame oil.

5. Sprinkle remaining ingredients on top (spring onion, parsley, seaweed, Sriracha to taste, and sesame seeds). Serve.

L

Lemon Raspberry Baked Oatmeal

Yield: 12

Ingredients:

- 4 cups old fashioned oats (gluten free certified if necessary)
- 2 1/3 cup unsweetened almond milk
- 2 teaspoons vanilla extract
- 2 teaspoons lemon zest (or more if you like)
- 1 ½ cups chopped raspberries (you could use fresh or frozen)
- 1 teaspoon ground cinnamon
- 1 teaspoon baking powder
- 1 tablespoon fresh lemon juice
- ½ teaspoon salt
- ¼ cup coconut sugar or brown sugar
- ¼ cup pure maple syrup

Method:

1. Start by pre-heating the oven to 375 F.
2. Add all dry ingredients to a large bowl and mix until combined. Add the wet ingredients and mix again. Save about ½ cup of raspberries to place on the top of the oatmeal.
3. Spray a 9×13 baking pan with cooking spray and pour in oatmeal mixture. Use a spatula to smooth out the top and place in the pre-heated oven.

4. Bake oatmeal until cooked through and mostly firm to the touch, about 30 minutes. Let cool for 10-15 minutes before cutting.

Note:

- Store the baked oatmeal in an airtight container in the refrigerator for up to 5 days.
- You can it cold, but if you want you can re-heat in the microwave for about 45 seconds. Or, re-heat in a 375 F oven for about 10 minutes.
- Baked oatmeal can be frozen in an airtight container for up to 3 months.
- If you want to make baked oatmeal cups out of this recipe, just use a ¼ scoop to scoop the batter into your oatmeal tin and bake at the same temperature for about 20-25 mins. This recipe will make about 12-15 oatmeal cups.

Lightened Up Cinnamon Roll Oatmeal

Yield: 2 servings

Ingredients:

- 2 cups old fashioned oats *(see note for quick cooking oats adaptations)*
- 2 cups low fat milk
- ½ teaspoon cinnamon

Cinnamon roll filling:

- 2 tablespoons brown sugar
- 1 tablespoon butter (unsalted)
- 1/8 teaspoon cinnamon

Cinnamon roll glaze:

- 2 tablespoons powdered sugar
- 1 tablespoon vanilla or plain greek yogurt
- dash of vanilla (optional)

Method:

1. First, pour the milk, oatmeal and cinnamon in a saucepan and turn the heat to medium high to bring the ingredients to a boil.
2. Turn down to medium low and simmer for 3-5 minutes.
3. Remove from the heat and place a lid on it.
4. Prepare the cinnamon roll filling by melting the butter and stirring in the cinnamon and brown sugar until combined.

5. Prepare the glaze by stirring together the Greek yogurt and powdered sugar.
6. Drizzle both over the top of the oatmeal in a bowl and sprinkle with cinnamon if desired.

Note:

- *To make this using quick cooking oats,* bring 1 cup of low-fat milk and cinnamon to a boil in a small saucepan. Stir in 1/2 cup oats and reduce the heat to medium; cook for 1 minute. Remove from the heat, cover and let stand for 2 to 3 minutes.

M

Mixed Vegetable Oatmeal

Serves: 4

Ingredients:

- 3 cups water
- 1 cup plain rolled oats
- 1 teaspoon oil
- 1 cup assorted bite size cut vegetables (you can use the froze ones too)
- 1 teaspoon salt
- ½ teaspoon cumin seeds
- ½ teaspoon cumin powder
- ¼ teaspoon turmeric powder

optional ingredients:

- ghee
- half boiled or hard-boiled eggs
- freshly cracked pepper
- finely chopped fresh cilantro leaves

Method:

1. First, place a heavy bottom pan on medium heat and drizzle the oil. When the oil heats up, scatter the cumin seeds and let it sizzle for a few seconds.
2. Drop the vegetables followed by ½ teaspoon salt, turmeric and cumin powder. Mix it and sauté for 1 minute.

3. Scatter the rolled oats, mix it around and pour the water. Sprinkle rest of the salt and bring the water to a boil. Then, bring the heat down to medium and let it simmer for 3 to 4 minutes or until the oats are cooked through and turns creamy.
4. Check for salt and add any, if required.
5. Serve warm by topping it with boiled eggs, drizzle of ghee, fresh cilantro and some freshly cracked black pepper.

Maple Bacon Oatmeal

Yield: 1

Ingredients:

- 3 slices bacon
- 1 cup old-fashioned rolled oats
- ½ cup milk or water
- ¼ cup maple syrup, plus more for drizzling
- kosher salt

Method:

1. First, cook bacon until crisp in a large skillet over medium heat, 6 minutes. Transfer to a paper towel-lined plate and let cool, then crumble.
2. In a medium saucepan over high heat, bring milk to a boil. Stir in oats and salt, reduce heat to low, and simmer until oats are tender and creamy, 5 minutes.
3. Add maple syrup and stir together until warm.
4. Serve oatmeal topped with crumbled bacon and drizzled with maple syrup.

Matcha Oatmeal

Servings: 4

Ingredients:

Matcha oats:

- 3 cups water
- 3 tablespoons maple syrup
- 1 ½ teaspoon vanilla extract
- 1 tablespoon matcha green tea powder
- 1 cup steel cut oats
- ¾ cup full-fat canned coconut milk
- pinch of salt

Toppings:

- 2 tablespoons cacao nibs
- 2 tablespoons goji berries
- 2 tablespoons shredded coconut (unsweetened)
- ¼ cup shelled pistachios
- maple syrup
- non-dairy milk, of choice

Method:

1. Start by combining water, coconut milk, and steel cut oats in a sauce pan. Cover. Bring to boil then reduce heat to low and simmer for 20 minutes, stirring occasionally.
2. Stir in matcha powder, maple syrup, vanilla extract, and salt.

3. Return cover and simmer for 5-10 more minutes until the liquid has evaporated and the oats are soft and creamy.
4. Divide oatmeal into 4 serving bowls and evenly top with pistachios, cacao nibs, goji berries, and coconut.
5. Serve with non-dairy milk of choice and maple syrup.

Masala Oatmeal

Servings: 4

Ingredients:

- 3 medium-large eggs
- 1 ½ cups vegetable broth
- 1-pint cherry tomatoes
- 1 cup water
- 1 cup quick oats
- 1 tablespoon madras curry paste
- 1 teaspoon canola oil
- 1 cup cilantro (whole leaves)
- 1 red chili (thinly sliced)
- 1 small onion (finely chopped)
- 1 garlic clove (minced)
- 1 teaspoon ginger (grated)
- ¼ teaspoon cumin seeds
- 1/8 teaspoon salt

Method:

1. First, whisk eggs with broth, water, oats and curry paste in a medium saucepan and set over medium-low. Cook, stirring often, until very creamy, about 15 min.
2. Heat a medium non-stick frying pan over medium. Add oil, then onion, tomatoes, garlic, ginger, cumin seeds and salt. Cook until tomatoes soften, 5 to 8 min.
3. Divide oatmeal among 4 bowls. Top with tomato mixture, cilantro and chili.
4. Serve and enjoy!

Mocha Crunch Steel-Cut Oatmeal

Servings: 2-4

Ingredients:

- 3 cups water
- 2 teaspoons instant espresso
- 1 - 2 tablespoons sugar or agave nectar
- 1 ½ tablespoons cocoa powder
- 1 cup steel-cut oats
- ¼ teaspoon salt
- ¼ cup roasted mixed nuts
- ¼ cup bittersweet chocolate chips
- milk or cream (to serve)

Method:

1. Bring water to a boil. Stir in oats, espresso, cocoa powder, and salt. Bring back to a boil and reduce heat to medium-low.
2. Simmer uncovered for 20 to 30 minutes, stirring frequently, until the oats reach your desired tenderness. Remove from the heat and stir in the sugar or agave nectar.
3. Meanwhile, while the oatmeal is cooking, roughly chop the mixed nuts and chocolate chips. Mix them in a small serving bowl.
4. When the oatmeal is ready, serve hot with milk or cream on the side, and sprinkled liberally with the nut and chocolate topping.

Miso Oatmeal Bowl

Servings: 1

Ingredients:

- 10 walnut halves
- 1 teaspoon miso paste (or to taste)
- 1 cup water
- ½ avocado (peeled, pitted, and cubed)
- ½ cup rolled oats
- ¼ cup fresh spinach (or to taste)
- 2 tablespoons chopped roasted seaweed, or to taste (optional)

Method:

1. First, bring water to a boil in a saucepan; add oats and miso paste. Cook for about 1 minute.
2. Add spinach, walnuts, and seaweed to oat mixture; cook, stirring occasionally, until oatmeal is desired consistency, about 5 minutes.
3. Pour oatmeal into a bowl and top with avocado.

Notes:

- You can use any miso paste available at most Asian markets. You may even add a bit of tofu just before serving for added protein.

N

Nutella Double Hot Chocolate Oatmeal

Servings: 6

Ingredients:

Oatmeal:

- 4 cups low fat/skim or almond milk
- 3 tablespoons unsweetened cocoa powder
- 2 tablespoons natural sweetener of choice/raw sugar
- 2 cups rolled oats (or quick oats)
- 2 tablespoons Nutella, a chocolate hazelnut spread (or any healthier hazelnut cacao spread)
- 1 tablespoon light butter (optional - butter ads a beautiful flavor to this oatmeal, but you can use coconut oil for a healthier option, or leave it out completely.)

Optional toppings:

- crushed hazelnuts
- chocolate chips
- extra nutella

Method:

1. Start by combining milk, Nutella, cocoa powder, sweetener/sugar and oats in a medium sized saucepan on medium - high heat until beginning to warm and steam. Stir to combine.

2. Bring to a gentle simmer and continue to stir occasionally. Once oats have fully absorbed the milk, take off heat. Add a little extra milk if oatmeal is too thick, until reaching your desired consistency,
3. Serve with your desired toppings.

No-Cook Overnight Oatmeal

Servings: 1

Ingredients:

- 2 teaspoons chia seeds
- 2 teaspoons honey
- 1 teaspoon ground cinnamon
- 1/3 cup milk
- ¼ cup rolled oats
- ¼ cup Greek yogurt
- ¼ cup fresh blueberries

Method:

1. Start by combining milk, oats, Greek yogurt, chia seeds, honey, and cinnamon in a ½-pint jar with a lid; cover and shake until combined.
2. Remove lid and fold in blueberries. Cover jar with lid.
3. Refrigerate oatmeal, 8 hours to overnight.

Notes:

- You can use almost any fruit - bananas, peaches, or any variety of berries work best.

O

Oats and Lentils

Servings: 8

Ingredients:

- 4 medium-large eggs
- 2 tablespoons (30 ml) finely chopped green onion
- 2 teaspoons (10 ml) unsalted butter
- 2 tablespoons (30 ml) canola oil
- 2 garlic cloves (minced)
- 1 cup (250 ml) sliced mushrooms
- 1 cup (250 ml) shredded aged cheddar or gruyère cheese
- 1 cup (250 ml) split red lentils
- 1 cup (250 ml) rolled oats
- ½ teaspoon (2 ml) dried thyme
- ½ teaspoon (2 ml) salt
- ½ cup (125 ml) diced onion
- ½ cup (125 ml) arugula
- ¼ teaspoon (1 ml) paprika
- pinch, red pepper flakes

Method:

1. First, add lentils to a medium saucepan and cover with 3 cups (750 mL) cold water.
2. Bring to a boil, cover, and cook over medium heat for 8 minutes. Stir in oats, thyme, salt, red pepper flakes, and an additional 1 ½ cup (375 mL) cold water.

3. Continue cooking over medium-high heat until the oats are tender and have thickened, about 7-9 minutes. Stir in additional water if the oats are too thick.
4. While the oats and lentils cook, heat oil in a medium skillet over medium-high heat. Add diced onion and cook for about 5 minutes, until softened.
5. Stir in garlic and mushrooms and cook until the mushrooms are golden and have released their liquid, about 5 minutes. Season to taste with salt and pepper.
6. Stir half of the shredded cheese and half of the green onion into the lentil mixture and season to taste with salt and pepper.
7. Melt butter in a large skillet and cook eggs to preferred doneness.
8. Divide lentil mixture into four bowls and top with the garlic mushrooms, fried egg, remaining cheese, green onion, arugula, and a pinch of paprika.

Oatmeal Parfait Cups

Servings: 12

Ingredients:

- 2 ripe bananas (sliced)
- 2 tablespoons honey
- 1 ¼ cups (125 g) rolled oats
- 1 teaspoon almond extract
- 1 teaspoon cinnamon
- full-fat yogurt (as needed)

Topping options:

- raspberry, as desired
- blueberry, as desired
- strawberry, as desired
- sliced almonds, as desired

Method:

1. Start by preheating oven to 350°F / 175°C.
2. In a medium bowl, mash the bananas into a paste.
3. Pour in the honey and almond extract, and mix until well combined.
4. Sprinkle on the rolled oats and cinnamon and mix until incorporated.
5. Evenly divide the oats into a greased 12-cup muffin tin.
6. Use your fingers to mold the oats into a cup shape in each of the muffin cups.
7. Bake for 15 minutes, until the oatmeal cups have set.

8. Remove the oatmeal cups from the muffin tin and place them on a serving plate.
9. Place a spoonful of yogurt in each cup and top with your choice of toppings.
10. Enjoy!

Oatmeal Waffles

Yield: 6 waffles

Ingredients:

- 6 tablespoons butter (melted)
- 3 teaspoons baking powder
- 2 medium-large eggs (lightly beaten)
- 2 tablespoons brown sugar
- 1 ½ cups whole milk
- 1 ½ cups all-purpose flour
- 1 cup quick-cooking oats
- ½ teaspoon ground cinnamon
- ¼ teaspoon salt
- assorted fresh fruit and yogurt of your choice

Method:

1. First, combine flour, oats, baking powder, cinnamon and salt in a large bowl; set aside.
2. In a small bowl, whisk eggs, milk, butter and brown sugar. Add to flour mixture; stir until blended.
3. Pour batter into a lightly greased waffle maker (amount will vary with size of waffle maker). Close lid quickly. Bake according to manufacturer's directions; do not open during baking. Use fork to remove baked waffle.
4. Top with fresh fruit and yogurt.

Oats Khichdi

Yield: 2-3

Ingredients:

- 3 cups water
- 1 cup oats
- 1 tablespoon ghee
- 1 teaspoon cumin seeds
- 1 green chili (chopped finely)
- 1 cup chopped vegetables (carrots, cauliflower, green peas)
- ½ cup moong dal
- ½ inch piece ginger (grated)
- ½ teaspoon turmeric
- salt to taste

Method:

1. First, soak the moong dal in some water till you are ready to add it to the recipe.
2. Heat ghee in a pressure cooker and add cumin seeds. Once the seeds start spluttering add ginger and green chilies.
3. Cook for a minute till the ginger is fragrant and add the chopped vegetables, turmeric, oats. Drain the moong dal and add it to the cooker along with 3 ½ cups water and salt.
4. Bring this to pressure and cook for two whistles. Let the pressure release naturally.
5. Serve hot topped with more ghee.

P

Peach Oatmeal

Servings: 1

Ingredients:

- 1/3 cup water
- ¼ cup old fashioned oats or ¼ cup quick oats
- ¼ cup sliced peaches in juice, canned (this works out to about 5 slices of peach and about 1/8 cup of juice)
- 1/8 teaspoon cinnamon
- 1/8 teaspoon butterscotch extract or 1⁄8 teaspoon vanilla extract
- ½ teaspoon Splenda sugar substitute (optional) or ½ teaspoon sugar (optional) or ½ teaspoon honey (optional)

Method:

1. First, cut up peach slices into small pieces.
2. In a bowl add oats, water, and peaches with juice.
3. Microwave in 500watt microwave for 2 minutes, stir, microwave for another 2 minutes, stir, then microwave in 1-minute intervals until cooked.
4. In a 1200watt microwave, microwave for 30 seconds, stir, microwave for another 30 seconds, stir, and then continue microwaving in 30 second intervals until cooked.
5. Once cooked, add cinnamon, butterscotch extract, and sweetener.

Note:

- This serving seems small since it is only ¼ cup of oats, but with the addition of peaches, it is quite filling, especially when served with a glass of milk; Feel free however, to increase one serving size to double this amount for a very hearty breakfast.

Pumpkin Spice Oatmeal

Servings: 1

Ingredients:

- 2 tablespoons pumpkin puree
- 1 tablespoon 100% maple syrup
- 1 teaspoon chia seed (dried)
- ½ teaspoon pure vanilla extract
- 1/3 cup old fashioned oats (uncooked)
- 1/3 cup unsweetened almond milk
- 1/3 cup water
- ¼ teaspoon pumpkin pie spice
- dash of salt to taste

Method:

1. First, stir together the chia seeds and dry oats in a microwave safe bowl.
2. Add water, almond milk, pumpkin puree, vanilla, spice and salt, and stir to combine.
3. Microwave* on high until boiling, for about 2.5 minutes (Microwave times may vary. Watch out for boil-over!)
4. Let sit in microwave for 5-10 minutes to thicken.
5. Remove from microwave and stir in maple syrup.
6. Add more toppings, if desired. Chopped dates, raisins or craisins would also be delicious.

Note:

- For those of you who shy away from microwaves, this can totally be made on the stovetop! Bring to a low boil and then reduce heat and simmer on low for a minute or two.

Pesto Caprese Oats

Servings: 1

Ingredients:

- 2 tablespoons part-skim mozzarella cheese (shredded)
- 1 tablespoon pesto (store-bought or homemade)
- 1 cup water
- 1 teaspoon extra virgin olive oil
- ½ cup old-fashioned rolled oats
- ¼ cup cherry tomatoes (sliced)
- ¼ teaspoon kosher salt

Homemade pesto:

- 2 cups fresh basil leaves
- 2 cloves garlic
- ½ cup parmesan cheese (fresh)
- ½ cup olive oil
- 1/3 cup pine nuts
- ¼ teaspoon salt
- ¼ teaspoon pepper

Method:

1. First, bring water to a boil in a medium saucepan over medium heat. Add oats and let cook for 5 minutes or until desired consistency.
2. In a separate skillet, place the olive oil over medium heat and cook the tomatoes until slightly crispy at the edges, about 5 minutes.
3. In a bowl, combine half of the cheese and cooked oats.

4. Top oatmeal with pesto, tomatoes, the rest of the cheese, and salt.

Homemade pesto:

1. Add the fresh basil leaves, garlic, pine nuts, parmesan cheese, salt, and pepper to the bowl of your food processor. Pulse 5 times until a coarse mixture form.
2. Turn the food processor on low and slowly add the olive oil in a steady stream.
3. Serve the pesto immediately or store in a small bowl covered with plastic wrap in the refrigerator.

Piña Colada Baked Oatmeal

Servings: 6

Ingredients:

- 2 cups rolled oats
- 2 medium-large eggs (room temperature)
- 1 teaspoon pure vanilla extract
- 1 cup finely minced fresh pineapple (or canned crushed pineapple)
- ¾ cup coconut milk (room temperature)
- ½ cup shredded coconut (plus additional for garnish, if desired)
- ½ cup salted cashew pieces or chopped macadamia nuts (plus additional for garnish, if desired)
- ½ teaspoon ground ginger
- ¼ teaspoon salt
- ¼ cup maple syrup
- ¼ cup coconut oil (melted and slightly cooled)

Method:

1. First, preheat oven to 350°F.
2. Lightly grease (or spray with nonstick cooking spray) an 8- by 8-inch glass baking dish.
3. Combine oats, coconut, cashew pieces, ground ginger, and salt in a large bowl. Mix in minced pineapple, coconut milk, eggs, maple syrup, and vanilla. Stir in coconut oil until all ingredients are well combined.
4. Spread mixture into prepared baking dish and bake for 25 to 30 minutes or until set and light golden brown on top. Allow to cool in the baking dish for at least 5 minutes before slicing.

5. Serve warm with optional garnishes, such as warm coconut milk drizzled over the top and additional cashew pieces.

Note:

- Either coconut milk from a carton (found in the refrigerated section of the grocery store) or canned coconut milk (found in the Asian foods section) will work in this recipe.
- The reason the milk and eggs should be at room temperate is because if they are cold, they will cause the coconut oil to re-solidify. To quickly warm everything up, you can put the whole eggs in a bowl of warm water for a few minutes and zap the milk in the microwave for 20 to 30 seconds.
- Reheat oatmeal by placing an individual serving on a plate, drizzling with a little coconut milk, and then heating in the microwave for about 30 seconds.

Pecan Persimmon Oatmeal

Servings: 3

Ingredients:

- 12 oz. persimmon, chopped with skin and seeds removed (½ cup)
- 6 teaspoons maple syrup
- 6 tablespoons pecans (chopped)
- 1 ½ teaspoons vanilla extract
- 1 cup rolled oats
- 1 cup unsweetened almond milk
- 1 cup water (may need more)
- ¾ teaspoon ground cinnamon
- ¾ teaspoon ground cardamom
- pinch of salt

Method:

1. First, place all ingredients, except for the pecans, in a small pot over medium heat.
2. Bring the mixture to a simmer and lower heat to low-medium, stirring occasionally.
3. Once the mixture starts to thicken up, stir in the pecan pieces.
4. Adjust recipe to your liking by adding more non-dairy milk/water or adding more maple syrup for sweetness.

Tips:

- You can use agave syrup instead of maple syrup, or switch the pecans out for seeds, and the almond milk out for soy, if you have a nut allergy.

Q

Quinoa Oatmeal

Servings: 2-4

Ingredients:

- 2 ½ cups non-dairy milk
- 2 cups water
- 2 tablespoons chia seeds
- 2 teaspoon cinnamon
- 1 cup quinoa
- ½ mango
- ½ banana
- ¼ cup pure maple syrup

Garnish:

- 1 tablespoon walnuts
- 1 tablespoon pecans
- 1 teaspoon cinnamon
- sliced fruit (optional)

Method:

1. First, chop walnuts or pecans and slice mango + banana then set both aside.
2. Toast quinoa in a pan for about 30 seconds, then add water. Bring to a boil, then reduce heat to a soft simmer on medium-low heat, and cover (keeping the lid ajar).

3. Cook for 15 minutes. Transfer the cooked & fluffy quinoa to your blender. Pour in the non-dairy milk, pure maple syrup, and cinnamon, and blend until smooth.
4. Add more pure maple syrup, if necessary, and re-blend.

Note:

- At this point you can add the blended quinoa back to the pot, if you'd like it hotter. If not, pour it directly into serving bowls and top with a sprinkle of cinnamon and chia seeds (1 tablespoon each bowl). Top with favorite sliced fruits like mango and banana.

R

Raspberry Oatmeal

Serves: 1

Ingredients:

- 1 teaspoon brown sugar
- 1 tablespoon maple syrup
- 1 cup skim milk (or your milk preference)
- ½ cup quick-cooking oats
- ¼ cup raspberries (frozen or fresh)

Method:

1. First, cook oats according to directions on the package.
2. When you add the oats to the milk, add the raspberries as well if you are using frozen. Otherwise, skip this step.
3. When oats are done, add remaining ingredients and mix well.
4. Serve and enjoy!

Raisin Oatmeal with Spices

Serves: 2

Ingredients:

- 2 tablespoons brown sugar
- 2 cups water
- 1 ½ cups rolled oats
- 1 pinch salt
- 1 teaspoon vanilla
- ½ teaspoon ground cinnamon
- 1/3 cup raisins
- ¼ teaspoon ground nutmeg

Method:

1. First, cook oats as directed on box, but mix the raisins and salt into the oats.
2. Remove from heat on stove or from microwave and add vanilla, cinnamon and nutmeg.
3. Sprinkle each bowl with brown sugar.
4. Enjoy!

S

Steel-Cut Oats Jambalaya

Servings: 8

Ingredients:

- 1-pound skinless, boneless chicken thighs (cut into ½-inch pieces)
- 12 ounces medium shrimp (peeled and deveined)
- 8 ounces andouille sausage (thinly sliced)
- 8 garlic cloves (minced)
- 2 ½ cups unsalted chicken stock (such as swanson)
- 2 tablespoons canola oil
- 2 cups white onion (chopped)
- 2 teaspoons paprika
- 2 bay leaves
- 1 ¼ teaspoons kosher salt (divided)
- 1 cup celery (diced)
- 1 cup green bell pepper (finely chopped)
- 1 cup red bell pepper (finely chopped)
- 1 teaspoon freshly ground black pepper
- 1 cup quick-cooking steel-cut oats (uncooked)
- 1 (14.5-ounce) can unsalted diced tomatoes, undrained
- ¾ teaspoon dried oregano
- ½ teaspoon ground red pepper
- ½ cup green onions (sliced)
- cooking spray

Method:

1. First, heat a Dutch oven over medium-high heat. Coat pan with cooking spray.
2. Add chicken to pan, and sprinkle with ¼ teaspoon salt; cook 4 minutes, turning to brown on all sides. Add sausage; sauté 2 minutes. Remove mixture from pan.
3. Add oil to pan; swirl to coat. Add white onion, celery, bell peppers, and garlic; sauté 8 minutes or until tender, scraping pan occasionally to loosen browned bits.
4. Stir in remaining 1 teaspoon salt, paprika, and next 4 ingredients (through bay leaves); sauté 1 minute. Add oats; cook 1 minute, stirring constantly. Add stock and tomatoes; bring to a boil. Reduce heat, and simmer, uncovered, 4 minutes.
5. Return chicken mixture to pan, and add shrimp; cook 5 minutes or until shrimp and oats are done and mixture thickens. Sprinkle with green onions.

Spinach, Tomato and Feta Oatmeal

Servings: 4

Ingredients:

- 2 cups old-fashioned rolled oats
- 2 tablespoons extra-virgin olive oil
- 2 teaspoons fresh dill (finely chopped)
- 2 scallions (thinly sliced)
- 2 teaspoons fresh lemon juice
- 1 5-ounce package fresh baby spinach
- 1 cup grape tomatoes (halved)
- ¾ cup feta (crumbled)
- kosher salt and freshly ground black pepper
- 1/8 teaspoon crushed red pepper (optional)
- kalamata olives (sliced, optional)

Method:

1. First, bring 4 cups water, lemon juice, 1 ¼ teaspoons salt, ½ teaspoon pepper and crushed red pepper if using to a boil in a large saucepan.
2. Stir in the oats, spinach and tomatoes, reduce the heat to medium and cook, stirring frequently, until the oats are just softened and the mixture is slightly thickened, about 7 minutes.
3. Remove the saucepan from the heat and stir in the feta, oil and dill.
4. Transfer the oatmeal to individual bowls and garnish with scallions and olives if using.
5. Serve and enjoy.

Sautéed Mushrooms, Arugula and Fried Egg Oatmeal

Serves: 4-5

Ingredients:

- 2 cup unsweetened almond milk
- 2 cup water
- 2 cup rolled oats
- ½ cup roasted red bell peppers (chopped)

Toppings:

- 8 ounces mushrooms (quartered)
- olive oil
- arugula
- medium-large eggs
- nutritional yeast or parmesan cheese
- flaky salt (or truffle salt) and cracked black pepper

Method:

1. First, bring water and almond milk to a boil on medium-high heat in a medium pot. Stir in oats and reduce to a simmer. Cook about 10 minutes until oats are tender and oatmeal is thickened. Season with a pinch of salt and stir in bell peppers.
2. In the meantime, heat a teaspoon or two of olive oil in a large skillet. Add mushrooms, a pinch of salt and black pepper and sauté until liquids are released and absorbed, about 8 minutes total. Set aside until ready to use.

3. Heat a little more olive oil in a skillet and fry eggs as desired.
4. Divide oatmeal between bowls. Top with a sprinkle of nutrition yeast, sautéed mushrooms, fried egg, a handful of arugulas.
5. Finish with a drizzle of olive oil, salt and freshly cracked black pepper.

Sweet Potato Pie Oats

Serves: 2

Ingredients:

- 3 tablespoons pumpkin maple pecan granola (or sub roasted pecans)
- 2-3 tablespoons brown sugar, maple syrup, or other sweetener of choice (like date paste)
- 1 ¾ cups water
- 1 cup rolled oats *(see note)*
- ½ cup sweet potato puree (1 small potato yield ~ ½ cup)
- ½ teaspoon ground cinnamon
- ½ tablespoon flaxseed meal (optional)

Method:

1. *To roast your sweet potato,* preheat oven to 400 F (204 F) and cut sweet potato in half and lightly coat with olive oil. Place flesh side down on a foil lined baking sheet and bake for 20-25 minutes or until soft and tender. This will depend on your size of potato. (Alternatively, pierce a few times with a fork and microwave for 4-5 minutes until tender.)
2. Once done, pull potatoes out of the oven and start your oats (see notes for steel cut directions). Bring water to a boil in a small saucepan. Once boiling add your oats and reduce heat to medium. Continue cooking until the oats have absorbed most of the water - about 5 minutes - stirring frequently.
3. In the meantime, mashed your sweet potato and measure out roughly ½ cup. Set aside.

4. Once your oats are just about done cooking (~5-minute mark), stir in sweet potato puree, sweetener of choice, cinnamon and flax seed and stir to combine. Taste and adjust flavor/seasonings as desired. To thin, add a splash of non-dairy milk (such as almond).
5. Divide oats between two serving bowls and sprinkle with Pumpkin Maple Pecan Granola (or roasted pecans). Add a drizzle of honey for more sweetness. Enjoy immediately. Best when fresh.

Notes:

- To make this recipe with steel-cuts oats, add ¾ cup raw steel cut oats to 1 ¼ cup boiling water, reduce heat to simmer and cover. It's recommended to cook for up to 25 minutes, but I prefer mine with a little more texture and only cook them for 15 minutes until they've just absorbed the water. If you prefer softer oats add ¼ more water in the beginning and continue cooking until the 20-25 minute mark.

Slow Cooker Peanut Butter and Jelly Oatmeal

Serves: 8

Ingredients:

- 4 cups water
- 4 cups milk
- 2 cups steel cut oats
- 1 teaspoon vanilla extract
- 1 teaspoon cinnamon
- 1 teaspoon coconut oil
- dash of salt
- ½-1 cup peanut butter
- ½-1 cup all fruit jelly spread
- ¼ cup chia seeds
- 1 ripe banana (cut into chunks, optional)

Method:

1. First, grease slow cooker pot with coconut oil (or cooking spray).
2. Add oats, chia seeds, water, milk, cinnamon, vanilla, dash of salt and banana if using in slow cooker.
3. Place lid on slow cooker and cook for 6 hours on low for firm texture and 8 hours on low for softer texture. Alternatively, cook on high for 3-4 hours.
4. In morning, mix in ½ cup peanut butter and ½ jelly into oatmeal.
5. Serve with an additional drizzle of peanut butter and jelly if desired.

Strawberries and Cream Oatmeal

Serves: 1

Ingredients:

- 1 cup milk or 1 cup soymilk
- ½ cup quick-cooking oats
- ½ cup strawberry
- ½ banana (optional)
- sugar or artificial sweetener (if desired)

Method:

1. Start by adding milk to oats in a deep bowl and microwave 3-5 minutes, depending on your microwave wattage and desired thickness. Watch carefully so it doesn't spill over the sides!
2. While oatmeal is cooking, wash and slice strawberries. Soft strawberries work well, so you may want to mash them a little bit, but that is up to you.
3. When cereal is done, stir strawberries and sliced banana (if using) into oatmeal. If desired, add a little sugar or splenda.

Notes:

- It is also good with a little vanilla extract if you are using plain milk, just to give it some flavor. Also, you may need to re-heat oatmeal a little before eating if your strawberries cool it down too much.

Sriracha Oatmeal

Serves: 2

Ingredients:

- 2 tablespoons extra-virgin olive oil
- 2 medium-large eggs (free-range and organic is best)
- 2 teaspoons fresh rosemary (minced)
- 2 cups water
- 1 cup rolled oats (not instant)
- 1 tablespoon bragg liquid aminos or low-sodium soy sauce
- 1 tablespoon sriracha (plus more for happy squirting)
- 1 clove garlic (minced)
- small handful whole cashews
- salt and freshly ground black pepper to taste

Method:

1. First, combine the oats, water, cashews, Liquid Aminos (or soy sauce), Sriracha, rosemary, and garlic in a small saucepan set over a medium heat. Bring it to a boil, cover, and lower the heat to maintain a gentle simmer.
2. Cook, stirring occasionally, until most of the liquid is absorbed and the oats are cooked through, about 5 minutes.
3. While the oats are cooking, heat the olive oil in a medium saucepan over a medium heat. Once the oil is hot, crack in the eggs. Sprinkle with salt and pepper. Cook the eggs to your desired consistency. For sunny side up, cook the egg (without flipping) until the

whites are set and the yolk is still jiggly, about 2 to 3 minutes.

4. Spoon out the oatmeal, and top each serving with a fried egg. Drizzle a little bit of leftover oil from the egg pan over the plated oatmeal.
5. Squirt additional Sriracha over all of it should you want a little extra heat.

Spicy Oatmeal and Kale

Serves: 2

Ingredients:

- 2 cloves garlic (minced, or more to taste)
- 2 leaves kale (stems discarded and leaves chopped, or more to taste)
- 2 tablespoons water (or more as needed)
- 1 tablespoon olive oil
- 1 cup quick-cooking oats
- 1 pinch red pepper flakes (or more to taste)
- salt to taste
- ½ cup water (or as needed)

Method:

1. Start by heating olive oil in a saucepan over medium heat.
2. Cook and stir garlic in hot oil until sizzling, about 30 seconds. Add kale and 2 tablespoons water to garlic, cover the saucepan with a lid, and cook until kale softens, 2 to 3 minutes.
3. Stir oats, red pepper flakes, and salt into kale mixture; pour in enough water to cover oats.
4. Cook and stir oats until desired consistency is reached, about 3 minutes.
5. Serve and enjoy!

Spiced Plum Baked Oatmeal

Yield: 1

Ingredients:

- 1 tablespoon shredded coconut
- 1 tablespoon slivered almonds
- 1 plum (diced)
- ½ cup rolled oats
- ½ teaspoon vanilla extract
- ½ teaspoon ground cinnamon
- ⅓ cup almond milk
- ¼ teaspoon baking powder
- ⅛ teaspoon blackstrap molasses
- pinch of ground ginger
- pinch of ground cloves
- pinch of salt
- 1 - 2 teaspoons maple syrup (optional)

Method:

1. First, preheat the oven to 350°F (180°C). Grease a small ramekin.
2. In a small bowl, combine the rolled oats, baking powder, cinnamon, ginger, cloves, salt, shredded coconut and slivered almonds.
3. Add the maple syrup, vanilla extract, blackstrap molasses and almond milk, and mix until well combined. Stir in the diced plum.
4. Transfer the mixture to the prepared ramekin. Bake for 20 - 25 minutes, or until the top is dry and golden brown. Enjoy!

T

Tiramisu Oatmeal

Serves: 1

Ingredients:

- 2 egg whites
- 2 teaspoons of instant coffee
- 2 teaspoons natvia natural sweetener or 1 tablespoon norbu sweetener
- 1 medium-large egg
- 1 teaspoon of cocoa powder
- ¾ cup milk of choice
- ½ cup rolled oats
- ½ teaspoon of salt

For the topping:

- 2 tablespoons cream cheese (can sub for 2% greek yogurt or ricotta)
- 1 tablespoon cocoa powder
- 1 teaspoon native natural sweetener or norbu sweetener
- milk to thin

Method:

1. First, whisk together the egg whites and whole egg in a small mixing bowl and set aside.
2. In a saucepan, combine the rolled oats, salt and milk of choice and heat until all the liquid is absorbed.

3. Add the egg mixture and whisk well into the oats. Continue stirring for approximately 2-3 minutes, until fully cooked and fluffy. Remove from the heat.
4. Add the instant coffee, cocoa powder and sweetener and mix until fully incorporated. Refrigerate mixture overnight.
5. Before eating, combine the cream cheese, cocoa and sweetener in a small bowl.
6. Slowly add in milk until a thick sauce is formed. Top on oatmeal pudding and dig in!

Notes:

- This oatmeal can be eaten warm, but it's best to make overnight for the true tiramisu flavor. Feel free to adjust amount of coffee based on preference- I like it really strong so opt for 2 teaspoons.

Tropical Coconut Oatmeal

Yield: 2

Ingredients:

- 1 ½ teaspoons vanilla extract
- 1 ¼ cups almond milk
- 1 cup old-fashioned rolled oats
- 1 cup canned coconut milk (light or full-fat)
- 1 tablespoon coconut sugar (or other sweetener of choice)
- 1 tablespoon chia seeds
- 1 cup pineapple (chopped)
- ¼ cup coconut flakes (toasted)*
- dash of salt

Method:

1. First, add oats and both milks in a medium saucepan.
2. Turn heat to high; bring to a boil. Reduce heat to simmer, stir, and cook for 5-7 minutes.
3. Add the sugar, chia seeds, vanilla, and salt. Stir until well combined. Cook until the oatmeal is your desired consistency, about 2-3 more minutes. Divide into two bowls.
4. Top each bowl with half of the pineapple chunks, half of the coconut flakes, and any other desired toppings.

Notes:

- To toast coconut flakes, preheat oven to 350°F. Spread coconut flakes in a single layer on a baking sheet. Bake for 5-7 minutes, until lightly browned.

Turmeric Chickpea Oats

Servings: 1

Ingredients:

- 1 heaping cup baby spinach or ½ cup frozen chopped spinach (rinsed well before adding)
- 1 heaping tablespoon nutritional yeast
- ½ cup rolled oats
- ½ cup unsweetened soy or almond milk
- ½ cup water
- scant ½ teaspoon turmeric (between ¼ and ½ teaspoon, depending on how much you like turmeric's flavor)
- ⅓ cup cooked chickpeas
- pinch salt
- pinch black pepper
- 1 tablespoon tahini, chopped cilantro or green onion tops, slivered almonds or chopped cashews, cubed tofu or tempeh, coconut bacon (optional additions)

Method:

1. *Shortcut method:* Place the oats, plant milk, water, salt, and pepper into a small bowl or saucepan. Cover and refrigerate overnight.
2. In the morning, bring oats to a boil in a small saucepan. When they're boiling, reduce the heat to a simmer, put the baby spinach on top of the oats, and cover the saucepan to let the spinach wilt (it'll only take a moment).

3. When the spinach is wilted down, stir it completely into the oats. (Alternately, add the frozen, chopped spinach after you reduce heat to a simmer and proceed with cooking).
4. *Add the turmeric.* Cook the oats, stirring frequently, until they're thick and creamy. It will only take a couple minutes, since you soaked the oats overnight.
5. Stir in the nutritional yeast, extra salt and/or pepper to taste, and any of the optional toppings/additions you like, along with an extra splash of plant milk if desired. Top with chickpeas and serve.
6. *Slightly longer method:* Add the oats, water, plant milk, salt, and pepper to a small saucepan and bring to a boil over medium heat. Reduce to a simmer and proceed cooking as instructed above. It'll just take a few minutes extra than if you had soaked the oats. Enjoy!

Notes:

- Recipe can be doubled, tripled, or quadrupled as needed!

Thin Mint Cookie Overnight Oats

Servings: 1

Ingredients:

- 2-4 teaspoons chocolate chips or mini chocolate chips
- 1 tablespoon unsweetened cocoa powder
- ½ cup rolled oats
- ½ tablespoon dutch or additional unsweetened cocoa powder
- ½ cup plain yogurt, such as coconut nondairy
- ¼ cup milk of choice
- ¼ cup nondairy creamer (for extra creaminess) or additional milk of choice
- 1/8 teaspoon salt
- 1/8 teaspoon to ¼ teaspoon pure peppermint extract
- sweetener of choice, to taste
- 1 tablespoon nut butter or melted coconut oil (optional)

Method:

1. First, be sure to use pure peppermint extract, not mint extract or imitation peppermint. You can use the full ¼ teaspoon for a strong peppermint flavor.
2. In a mason jar or any container with a lid, stir all ingredients very well. Seal the lid tightly, and shake vigorously. Refrigerate overnight.
3. The next day, simply take off the lid and enjoy. (If you prefer hot overnight oats, feel free to heat them up at

this time.) Sweeten as desired, either before or after letting sit overnight.

Triple-Chocolate Cranberry Oatmeal Cookies

Yield: about 30

Ingredients:

- 10 tablespoons (1 ¼ sticks) unsalted butter (room temperature)
- 2 ounces milk chocolate or white chocolate, chopped (for drizzling)
- 1 medium-large egg
- 1 teaspoon vanilla extract
- 1 cup old-fashioned oats
- 1 cup all-purpose flour
- ½ teaspoon baking soda
- ½ teaspoon cinnamon
- ½ cup sugar
- ½ cup (packed) golden brown sugar
- ½ cup semisweet chocolate chips
- ½ cup milk chocolate chips
- ½ cup white chocolate chips
- ½ cup coarsely chopped fresh or frozen cranberries
- ¼ teaspoon salt

Method:

1. Start by positioning rack in center of oven and preheat to 350°F.
2. Line 2 large rimmed baking sheets with parchment paper. Whisk flour, baking soda, cinnamon, and salt in medium bowl to blend.

3. Using electric mixer, beat butter and both sugars in large bowl until smooth. Beat in egg and vanilla. Add flour mixture and oats and stir until blended. Stir in all chocolate chips and cranberries.
4. Drop batter by rounded tablespoonfuls onto prepared sheets, 2 inches apart. Bake cookies, 1 sheet at a time, until edges are light brown, about 16 minutes. Cool on sheets 5 minutes. Transfer to rack; cool completely.
5. Stir chopped milk chocolate in top of double boiler until melted and smooth. Using small spoon, drizzle melted chocolate over cookies in zigzag pattern.
6. Let stand until milk chocolate sets, about 1 hour. (Can be made 2 days ahead. Store in airtight container at room temperature)

Tahini Chocolate Chip Oatmeal with Caramelized Bananas

Yield: 1

Ingredients:

To make the stovetop oatmeal:

- ½ cup (50 g) old fashioned oats (use gluten-free if needed)
- 2/3 cup water plus more if it's too thick
- dash of sea salt
- drizzle of non-dairy milk such as almond, cashew or coconut

For the caramelized banana:

- 1 teaspoon coconut oil or use coconut oil cooking spray
- 1 banana, sliced into ½ inch thick rounds (or cut in half then slice lengthwise, don't cut them too thin or they'll turn to mush)
- generous sprinkle of coconut sugar or drizzle of maple syrup
- sprinkle of cinnamon (optional)

For topping the oatmeal:

- 2 tablespoons tahini
- 1-2 tablespoons dairy-free chocolate chips
- 1-2 tablespoons chopped pecans or other chopped nuts (optional)

Method:

To make the stovetop oatmeal:

1. Bring the water to a boil in a small saucepan then reduce heat to bring down to a simmer.
2. Add the oats and cook for about 5 minutes, stirring occasionally.
3. Stir in a pinch of sea salt, scoop into a bowl and top with a drizzle of plant-based milk, tahini, chocolate chips and the caramelized banana.

To make the caramelized banana:

1. Heat the oil in a non-stick pan or medium-high heat (or heat and spray pan with non-stick cooking spray.)
2. Add the sugar or maple syrup. You just want enough so each banana gets lightly coated in sweetener. You can add a sprinkling of cinnamon here if you're using.
3. Add the banana rounds and cook for 3-4 minutes until they're getting puffy and turning golden brown underneath. You can check them carefully with a fork or spatula. The time will vary depending on your stove so be careful not to burn them.
4. Gently flip them over and cook for about 1 more minute to brown the other side. Remove from heat and spoon over your bowl of oatmeal.

V

Vegan Oatmeal

Servings: 2

Ingredients:

- 2 tablespoons good maple syrup
- 1 cup rolled oats
- 1 cup oat milk, soy milk, or other non-dairy milk of your choice
- 1 cup water
- ½ teaspoon vanilla extract
- ½ teaspoon ground cinnamon
- pinch of ground nutmeg
- fresh or frozen berries *(see note)*
- peanut butter
- ground flaxseed
- unsweetened desiccated coconut

Method:

1. First, combine the oats, milk, water, maple syrup, vanilla, cinnamon, and nutmeg in a small pot.
2. Bring to a boil over medium-high heat, then reduce to a gentle simmer. Cook, stirring occasionally, for a few minutes, until the porridge is soft and a little thinner than you'd like it. It will thicken quickly as it cools.
3. To serve, divide oatmeal between two bowls and top with berries, a spoonful of peanut butter, and a sprinkling of flaxseed and coconut.

Notes:

- You can put a big handful or two of frozen berries into a bowl and heat them in the microwave until really syrupy (a couple of minutes on high power, depending on your microwave), then pour the syrup over the oatmeal. But regular old fresh or defrosted berries work beautifully, too.

W

Whole-Wheat Crepes

Servings: 4

Ingredients:

- 3 medium-large eggs
- 1 cup whole-wheat flour
- 1 cup milk
- 1 tablespoon honey
- 1 teaspoon pure vanilla extract
- 1 tablespoon butter (melted, plus extra for cooking)
- ¾ cup water
- ¼ teaspoon salt

Method:

1. First, put all ingredients in blender and mix well. Let stand about 15 minutes.
2. Melt and swirl around a small pat of butter in an 8 or 10-inch frying pan over medium heat.
3. Angle pan and pour enough batter on one side to thinly and evenly cover the pan. Very quickly swirl the batter around to cover the pan in one thin layer.
4. Immediately use your cooking spatula to push down the thin edges of the crepe around the perimeter.
5. After about 1 minute (and once it is golden brown on the bottom) carefully flip it over without tearing the crepe.
6. Fry for 1 more minute on the other side (until it is golden brown as well) and then roll up each crepe.

7. Serve with 100% pure maple syrup.

Z

Zucchini Oats with Basil Pesto

Servings: 2

Ingredients:

- 2 medium-large eggs
- 1 ½ teaspoons garlic (minced)
- 1 cup microgreens
- 1 cup oats
- 1 zucchini
- 1 package (71 grams) basil, fresh (this is about 4 cups, unpacked)
- 1 tablespoon lemon juice
- 1 tablespoon nutritional yeast
- ¾ teaspoon salt
- ½ cup cherry or small heirloom tomatoes
- ½ cup pine nuts
- ½ teaspoon black pepper
- roasted red pepper flakes, to taste

Method:

1. First, soft boil your eggs. Fill a saucepan high enough with water to cover eggs. Bring to a boil. Add eggs, cover, and turn heat down to low. Simmer for 6 minutes. Then remove from heat, run eggs under cold water to stop them from cooking, and refrigerate until ready to peel.

2. Bring one cup of water to boil in a small saucepan. Add oats, stir, and reduce heat to medium low. Simmer for 3 minutes.
3. Shred your zucchini on a cheese grater. Add into the pot with oatmeal, stir, and simmer for another 2 minutes.
4. Combine pesto ingredients in a small blender and blend until smooth.
5. Chop tomatoes into quarters.
6. Swirl a dollop of the pesto (1-2 tablespoons) into your oatmeal and stir well.
7. Peel your soft-boiled eggs.
8. Divide oatmeal between two bowls. Top each with tomatoes, microgreens, and a soft-boiled egg. Top with additional pesto and red pepper flakes.

Notes:

- Barley and farro would also work well in this recipe.
- Parmesan cheese can be substituted for nutritional yeast if you prefer.
- The recipe can easily be cut in half to make a single serving. Leftovers do not store well.
- Note that the pesto portion of this recipe makes four servings. Extra pesto can be stored in the fridge for a few days. Leftovers can be used on pasta. Pesto also freezes well.

Conclusion

I want to thank you once again for purchasing this book.

Oatmeal has a variety of beneficial health influences on humans. For a start it lowers cholesterol levels. Oatmeal has a specific type of fiber namely – beta-glucan, which lowers total cholesterol levels in the organism. According to some studies oats also oats helps prevent heart disease.

Antioxidants that oats have, called avenanthramides, don't let free radicals to damage LDL cholesterol and, with that, reduce the risk of cardiovascular diseases like atherosclerosis. Fibers in oatmeal also make you feel full after the finished meal which prevents you from overeating and can even reduce weight.

Your body digests and absorbs oatmeal slowly, which keeps you feeling full and you don't feel the need to eat more. Insolvable fibers help indigestion and prevent constipation. Beta-glucan fiber also enhances the human immune system and its response to bacterial infection.

It helps neutrophils (immune cells) find the place of an infection and it even helps them fight it. Fibers also prevent sugar to enter the bloodstream to fast which lowers the risk of Type 2 diabetes and even lowers the level of sugar in blood at those that already have Type 2 diabetes. A study performed in Finland showed that children which were earlier introduced to oatmeal are less likely to develop persistent asthma.

Thank you and all the best.

Other Books by Grizzly Publishing

"Jamaican Cookbook: Traditional Jamaican Recipes Made Easy"

https://www.amazon.com/dp/B07B68KL8D

"Brazilian Instant Pot Cookbook: Delicious Pressure Cooked Meals Made Fast and Easy"

https://www.amazon.com/dp/B078XBYP89

"Norwegian Cookbook: Traditional Scandinavian Recipes Made Easy"

https://www.amazon.com/dp/B079M2W223

"Casserole Cookbook: Delicious Casserole Recipes From Around The World"

https://www.amazon.com/dp/B07B6GV61Q

Lightning Source UK Ltd.
Milton Keynes UK
UKHW020235100222
398450UK00003B/176